Dedicated to all the curious minds who have ever wondered about the mysteries of time and memory, and who seek to understand the intricacies of the human experience. May this book inspire you to keep exploring, asking questions, and seeking answers.

THE PARADOXES OF TIME: UNRAVELING THE MYSTERIES OF THE FOURTH DIMENSION

SHIVAM GOEL

Made with ♥ on the Notion Press Platform
www.notionpress.com

Contents

Foreword

Foreword

As we journey through life, we are constantly aware of the passage of time. From the rise and fall of the sun, to the milestones in our personal lives, time is a ubiquitous presence that shapes our understanding of the world and our place in it. Yet, despite its omnipresence, the nature of time remains a mystery that has confounded philosophers, scientists, and mathematicians for centuries.

In this book, "The Paradoxes of Time: Unraveling the Mysteries of the Fourth Dimension," the author delves into the complex and often paradoxical nature of time, exploring its various aspects and interpretations. From the scientific theories of relativity and quantum mechanics, to the philosophical musings of some of the greatest minds in history, this book offers a comprehensive overview of the many questions and debates surrounding time.

The author does not shy away from the challenges that come with attempting to understand such a complex and abstract concept, and instead embraces them, presenting the reader with a thought-provoking and engaging journey through the mysteries of time. Whether you are a scientist, a philosopher, or simply someone who has a love of learning, this book is sure to deepen your appreciation of the wonders of time and its impact on our lives.

So, if you are ready to embark on a journey through the paradoxes of time, grab a copy of this book and let the author be your guide. I am confident that you will find the experience both enlightening and enjoyable.

Preface

Preface

The concept of time has captivated the human imagination for millennia. It is a fundamental aspect of our existence, and yet it remains one of the most mysterious and elusive ideas we have ever encountered. From ancient philosophers pondering the nature of time, to modern scientists exploring its implications in the realm of physics, time continues to be a subject of intense fascination and study.

In this book, "The Paradoxes of Time: Unraveling the Mysteries of the Fourth Dimension," I explore the many facets of time, from its philosophical roots to its scientific implications. This book is not a definitive answer to the many questions surrounding time, but rather a comprehensive overview of the current state of our understanding and the ongoing debates that exist.

In writing this book, I have tried to present the material in a clear and accessible way, so that it may be enjoyed by readers of all levels of understanding. Whether you are an expert in the field, or simply someone who has a passing interest in the subject, I believe that you will find something of value within these pages.

My goal in writing this book is to contribute to the ongoing conversation about time, and to encourage readers to think critically and creatively about this elusive concept. Whether you come away from this book with a deeper understanding of time, or with a renewed sense of mystery, I hope that you will find the journey both enlightening and enjoyable.

So, I invite you to join me as we explore the paradoxes of time, and attempt to unravel the mysteries of this fourth dimension.

Acknowledgements

Acknowledgements

Writing a book is a journey that involves many people along the way. This book would not have been possible without the support, encouragement, and inspiration of the following individuals.

First and foremost, I would like to express my gratitude to my family. Their unwavering support and encouragement throughout this process has been invaluable. I would also like to thank my friends, who have always been a source of inspiration and support.

I would also like to extend my heartfelt thanks to the experts and scholars in the field of time and its related disciplines who have generously shared their knowledge and insights with me. Their expertise has been an essential part of this book and I am deeply grateful for their contributions.

I would also like to thank my editors and publishers for their support and guidance throughout this process. Their insights, expertise, and commitment to excellence have been invaluable in helping to bring this book to life.

Finally, I would like to acknowledge my readers. Your interest in the subject of time is what motivates me to continue exploring its many mysteries and paradoxes. I hope that this book will inspire you to continue your own journey of discovery and learning.

So, thank you to all of you who have supported me in this journey. Your contributions have been invaluable and I am deeply grateful for your support.

Prologue

Prologue

Time is a mysterious and paradoxical concept that has captivated human imagination for centuries. It is both the foundation of our daily lives and the source of some of the most perplexing questions in science and philosophy.

Despite its ubiquity, time remains one of the least understood concepts in the universe. It is both a physical entity and a human construct, and its effects can be observed in everything from the aging of living organisms to the movement of celestial bodies.

In this book, we will delve into the many paradoxes of time, exploring its mysterious properties and attempting to unravel its secrets. From the relationship between time and gravity, to the possibility of time travel, we will examine the latest research and theories on this elusive subject.

With the help of experts and scholars in the field, we will explore the boundaries of our current understanding of time, and consider what the future may hold for this enigmatic concept. Whether you are a seasoned physicist or simply someone with a curious mind, "The Paradoxes of Time: Unraveling the Mysteries of the Fourth Dimension" is a must-read for anyone seeking to deepen their understanding of this fascinating and elusive concept.

CHAPTER ONE

If time travel was possible, what ethical considerations would need to be taken into account

Time travel, once thought to be the stuff of science fiction, is now a widely discussed topic in both the scientific and philosophical communities. While the feasibility of time travel remains a topic of debate, many scientists and philosophers are considering the potential implications if time travel were to become a reality. The idea of time travel has captured the imagination of people for centuries, and with advancements in science and technology, it has become a topic of serious discussion and study. While the feasibility of time travel is still a matter of debate, it is important to consider the ethical implications of such a technology. Time travel raises many questions about the nature of time, causality, and the consequences of our actions. It would have far-reaching consequences for our understanding of the world and our place in it. However, before we embark on such a journey, it is important to consider the ethical implications of this technology. If time travel were possible, it could open up new avenues for exploration and discovery, but it could also have profound ethical implications. This Chapter aims to explore the ethical considerations that would need to be taken into account if time travel were possible.

Body:

The Butterfly Effect: One of the most fundamental principles of time travel is the butterfly effect, which states that small changes in the past can have a significant impact on the future. This raises ethical questions about the potential consequences of time travel, such as altering historical events and creating unintended consequences.

The Ethics of Interference: Time travelers would inevitably face the question of whether or not to interfere with events in the past. This raises ethical considerations about the morality of altering historical events and the potential consequences of these actions. For example, would it be ethical to prevent a tragedy from occurring if the outcome is unknown?

The Responsibility of Time Travelers: If time travel were possible, those who engage in time travel would have a significant responsibility to consider the potential consequences of their actions. This includes the responsibility to not alter historical events and to act in a manner that is consistent with ethical principles.

The Paradox of Time Travel: Time travel raises the question of paradoxes, such as the grandfather paradox, where a time traveler would potentially be able to change the course of their own history. This raises ethical considerations about the possibility of creating paradoxes and the impact these paradoxes could have on the timeline.

The Potential for Abuse: Time travel could be used for malicious purposes, such as altering historical events for personal gain or altering the course of history for political purposes. This raises ethical considerations about the need to regulate time travel and prevent its abuse.

The Ethics of Knowledge: Time travel could potentially provide access to knowledge that was previously unknown or unavailable. This raises ethical considerations about the responsible use of this knowledge, as well as the potential consequences of using it. For example, would it be ethical to use knowledge gained through time travel for personal gain or to advance one's own interests?

The Concept of Free Will: Time travel raises questions about the concept of free will and the ability of individuals to make choices and determine their own destiny. This raises ethical considerations about the impact of time travel on free will and the potential for time travelers to interfere with the choices of others.

The Impact on Society: Time travel could have a profound impact on society and the way people live their lives. This raises ethical considerations about the need to ensure that time travel is used in a way that is consistent with the values and goals of society. For example, would it be ethical to use time travel to change the outcome of an election or to alter the course of historical events?

The Ethical Implications of Time Travel on the Environment: Time travel could potentially impact the environment and the balance of nature. This raises ethical considerations about the need to ensure that time travel is used in a way that is consistent with the goal of preserving the environment and protecting the planet.

The Responsibility to Future Generations: Time travel could impact future generations, as the consequences of our actions in the past could ripple through time. This raises ethical considerations about the responsibility of time travelers to act in a way that protects the interests of future generations.

The Ethics of Historical Research: Time travel would provide researchers with unprecedented access to the past, allowing them to study historical events and cultures in a way that was previously impossible. This raises ethical considerations about the responsibility of researchers to maintain the integrity of historical events and to respect the privacy and dignity of individuals from the past.

The Ethics of Commercialization: Time travel could become a commodity and be used for commercial purposes. This raises ethical considerations about the need to regulate the commercialization of time travel and to ensure that it is not used for profit at the expense of society or the environment.

The Ethics of Access: Time travel raises questions about who should have access to this technology. This raises ethical considerations about the need to ensure that time travel is used in a way that is equitable and consistent with the principles of social justice. For example, would it be ethical to restrict access to time travel based on social class, race, or gender?

The Responsibility to Preserve the Past: Time travel could potentially impact the preservation of historical sites and artifacts. This raises ethical considerations about the need to ensure that time travel is used in a way that protects the cultural heritage of humanity and preserves the past for future generations.

The Ethics of Temporal Responsibility: Time travel raises questions about the temporal responsibility of time travelers. This raises ethical considerations about the need to ensure that time travelers are held accountable for their actions in the past, as well as the potential consequences of their actions in the future.

The Ethics of Interference: Time travel raises questions about the impact of time travelers on the course of history. This raises ethical considerations about the need to ensure that time travelers do not interfere with the natural course of events, as this could have unintended consequences.

The Responsibility to Respect the Past: Time travel would provide access to the past, allowing us to observe and interact with historical events and individuals. This raises ethical considerations about the need to respect the past and to ensure that the privacy and dignity of individuals from the past are not violated.

The Ethics of Responsibility: Time travel raises questions about the responsibility of time travelers for their actions in the past. This raises ethical considerations about the need to ensure that time travelers are held accountable for their actions and the potential consequences of their actions in the future.

The Ethics of Time Paradoxes: Time travel raises questions about the concept of causality and the possibility of time paradoxes. This raises ethical considerations about the need to ensure that time travelers do not create paradoxes or alter the course of events in a way that is inconsistent with the laws of physics and the nature of time.

The Responsibility to Protect the Present: Time travel raises questions about the impact of time travelers on the present. This raises ethical considerations about the need to ensure that time travelers do not alter the present in a way that is harmful or disruptive.

The Ethics of Knowledge and Information: Time travel would provide access to vast amounts of knowledge and information about the past. This raises ethical considerations about the need to ensure that the information obtained through time travel is used in a responsible and ethical manner, and that it is not used for malicious or harmful purposes.

The Responsibility to Ensure Accuracy: Time travel raises questions about the accuracy of historical events and information. This raises ethical considerations about the need to ensure that the information obtained through time travel is accurate and reliable, and that it is not distorted or misrepresented.

The Ethics of Exploitation: Time travel raises questions about the exploitation of individuals and cultures from the past. This raises ethical considerations about the need to ensure that time travelers do not exploit or take advantage of individuals and cultures from the past for personal gain.

The Responsibility to Respect Cultural Diversity: Time travel raises questions about the impact of time travelers on cultural diversity. This raises ethical considerations about the need to ensure that time travelers respect the cultural diversity of individuals and cultures from the past, and that they do not interfere with or alter cultural practices or beliefs.

he Responsibility to Ensure Safe Time Travel: Time travel raises questions about the safety of the time traveler and any individuals they may encounter in the past or future. This raises ethical considerations about the need to ensure that time travel is safe for all involved and that the risks are understood and minimized.

The Ethics of Changing the Past: Time travel raises questions about the impact of time travelers on the past and the possibility of changing historical events. This raises ethical considerations about the need to ensure that time travelers do not change the past in a way that is harmful or disruptive, and that they do not alter the course of history in a way that is inconsistent with ethical principles.

The Responsibility to Protect the Future: Time travel raises questions about the impact of time travelers on the future. This raises ethical considerations about the need to ensure that time travelers do not alter the future in a way that is harmful or disruptive, and that they do not create unintended consequences for future generations.

The Ethics of Time Travel for Personal Gain: Time travel raises questions about the motivations of time travelers, and whether time travel could be used for personal gain or advantage. This raises ethical considerations about the need to ensure that time travel is not used for malicious or harmful purposes, and that it is not used to exploit or take advantage of individuals or cultures.

The Responsibility to Ensure Ethical Time Travel: Time travel raises questions about the responsibility of those who control and regulate time travel. This raises ethical considerations about the need to ensure that time travel is regulated in a way that is consistent with ethical principles, and that it is used in a responsible and ethical manner.

The Responsibility to Ensure Time Travel Equality: Time travel raises questions about access and equity, and whether time travel would be available to all people or just a privileged few. This raises ethical considerations about the need to ensure that time travel is available to all individuals, regardless of their socioeconomic status, race, or other factors.

The Ethics of Time Travel for Scientific Research: Time travel raises questions about the use of time travel for scientific research and the impact this may have on individuals and cultures from the past and present. This raises ethical considerations about the need to ensure that scientific research is conducted in a responsible and ethical manner, and that the interests of all stakeholders are taken into account.

The Responsibility to Ensure the Integrity of Historical Events: Time travel raises questions about the impact of time travelers on historical events, and the possibility of altering or distorting these events. This raises ethical considerations about the need to ensure that historical events are preserved in their original form, and that they are not altered or distorted by time travelers.

The Ethics of Time Travel for Military Purposes: Time travel raises questions about the use of time travel for military purposes, and the impact this may have on individuals and cultures from the past and present. This raises ethical considerations about the need to ensure that military time travel is used in a responsible and ethical manner, and that it is not used to harm or exploit individuals or cultures.

The Responsibility to Ensure Time Travel Security: Time travel raises questions about security, and the risk of individuals or organizations using time travel for malicious or harmful purposes. This raises ethical considerations about the need to ensure that time travel is secure, and that measures are in place to prevent individuals or organizations from using time travel for malicious or harmful purposes.

In conclusion, if time travel were to become a reality, a number of ethical considerations would need to be taken into account. These considerations include the butterfly effect, the ethics of interference, the responsibility of time travelers, the paradox of time travel, and the potential for abuse. The ethical implications of time travel are complex and far-reaching, and it is essential that these considerations be addressed in a responsible and thoughtful manner. The ethical implications of time travel are complex and far-reaching, and it is essential that these considerations be addressed in a responsible and thoughtful manner. Whether time travel is ever possible remains to be seen, but it is important to consider the potential consequences of this technology in advance, in order to ensure that it is used in a way that is consistent with ethical principles and protects the interests of all.

CHAPTER TWO

How does time affect the aging process of living organisms?"

Introduction:

Aging is a natural biological process that affects all living organisms, and time plays a crucial role in the aging process. The rate of aging can vary greatly among species and even within individuals of the same species. This chapter will examine the ways in which time affects the aging process of living organisms, and explore the scientific theories and mechanisms underlying the aging process.

Body:

The Role of Time in the Aging Process: Time is a key factor in the aging process, as the accumulation of time leads to the gradual decline of physical and biological functions. Over time, cells and tissues in the body undergo changes that lead to the breakdown of cellular and molecular functions, ultimately resulting in aging.

The Role of Genetics in the Aging Process. While time is a key factor in the aging process, genetics also play a crucial role in determining the rate of aging. Certain genetic factors can affect the rate of aging and determine how long an organism can live. For example, certain genetic mutations can lead to a longer lifespan, while others may lead to a shorter lifespan.

The Role of Environmental Factors in the Aging Process: Environmental factors can also play a role in the aging process, and can either accelerate or slow down the rate of aging. Exposure to environmental stressors such as pollution, radiation, and oxidative stress can cause damage to cells and tissues, leading to an increased rate of aging. On the other hand, exposure to a healthy diet, regular exercise, and a low-stress environment can help to slow down the rate of aging.

The Role of Free Radicals in the Aging Process: Free radicals are highly reactive molecules that can cause damage to cells and tissues in the body, leading to the breakdown of cellular and molecular functions and an increased rate of aging. Over time, the accumulation of free radicals in the body can lead to oxidative stress and cellular damage, leading to the aging process.

The Role of Inflammation in the Aging Process: Inflammation is a normal response of the body to injury or infection, but chronic inflammation can play a role in the aging process. Chronic inflammation can cause damage to cells and tissues in the body, leading to the breakdown of cellular and molecular functions and an increased rate of aging.

The Role of Telomeres in the Aging Process: Telomeres are the protective end caps on the chromosomes that shorten as cells divide over time. The gradual shortening of telomeres has been linked to the aging process, as well as an increased risk of age-related diseases such as cancer, heart disease, and cognitive decline. Research has shown that factors such as stress, oxidative stress, and inflammation can accelerate the rate of telomere shortening, leading to an increased rate of aging.

The Role of Mitochondria in the Aging Process: Mitochondria are the powerhouses of the cell, and they play a key role in the aging process. As cells age, the number and function of mitochondria decline, leading to a decreased ability of cells to produce energy. This can cause cellular damage, leading to the aging process. In addition, the accumulation of damaged mitochondria can lead to oxidative stress, further contributing to the aging process.

The Role of Hormones in the Aging Process: Hormones play a crucial role in regulating various biological processes in the body, and changes in hormone levels can affect the rate of aging. For example, declining levels of hormones such as estrogen and testosterone have been linked to the aging process and an increased risk of age-related diseases. On the other hand, hormone replacement therapy has been shown to have anti-aging effects in some cases.

The Role of Lifestyle Factors in the Aging Process: Lifestyle factors can also play a role in the aging process, and can either accelerate or slow down the rate of aging. Factors such as diet, exercise, stress management, and adequate sleep have been shown to impact the aging process, and adopting a healthy lifestyle can help to slow down the rate of aging.

Conclusion on the Role of Time in the Aging Process: In conclusion, time plays a crucial role in the aging process, and the rate of aging is influenced by a complex interplay of factors including genetics, environmental factors, free radicals, inflammation, telomeres, mitochondria, hormones, and lifestyle factors. Understanding the ways in which these factors interact to affect the aging process is crucial for developing interventions to slow down the rate of aging and improve health outcomes for individuals as they age.

The Free Radical Theory of Aging: Free radicals are unstable molecules that can damage cells and tissues over time, leading to the aging process. Antioxidants, which neutralize free radicals, can help to slow down the rate of aging by reducing oxidative stress and cellular damage.

The Role of Inflammation in the Aging Process: Chronic low-grade inflammation has been linked to the aging process, as well as an increased risk of age-related diseases. This type of inflammation is thought to arise from environmental factors such as diet and lifestyle, and can have a detrimental effect on the body over time.

The Influence of Genetics on the Aging Process: Genetics plays a role in determining an individual's lifespan, and can influence the rate of aging. Certain genetic mutations and variations have been linked to a shorter lifespan and a more rapid rate of aging, while others have been linked to a longer lifespan and a slower rate of aging.

The Role of Environmental Factors in the Aging Process: Environmental factors such as exposure to toxins, radiation, and stress can also influence the rate of aging. These factors can cause oxidative stress, inflammation, and cellular damage, leading to the aging process. On the other hand, exposure to certain environmental factors, such as exposure to sunlight, has been shown to have anti-aging effects.

The Interplay of Telomeres, Mitochondria, Hormones, and Lifestyle Factors: The aging process is a complex interplay of multiple factors, and the impact of each factor is interdependent. For example, the shortening of telomeres can be influenced by oxidative stress, inflammation, and lifestyle factors, while changes in hormone levels can affect both telomere length and mitochondrial function. By understanding the interplay of these factors, researchers can develop more effective strategies for slowing down the rate of aging and improving health outcomes for individuals as they age.

The Connection Between Aging and Age-Related Diseases: Age-related diseases such as heart disease, Alzheimer's disease, and cancer become more prevalent with increasing age, and are thought to be connected to the aging process. These diseases can also contribute to the aging process by causing oxidative stress, inflammation, and cellular damage.

The Importance of Mitochondrial Maintenance in the Aging Process: Maintaining the health and function of mitochondria is crucial for slowing down the rate of aging. Strategies such as increasing antioxidant intake, reducing oxidative stress, and promoting healthy mitochondrial function through exercise and a balanced diet can help to slow down the rate of aging.

The Role of Epigenetics in the Aging Process: Epigenetics refers to changes in gene expression that occur without changes to the underlying DNA sequence. These changes can be influenced by factors such as diet, lifestyle, and environmental exposure, and can have a lasting impact on the aging process. For example, certain lifestyle factors can lead to changes in gene expression that promote healthy aging, while others can lead to changes that accelerate the rate of aging.

The Importance of Sleep in the Aging Process: Sleep is a critical component of health and well-being, and it plays a role in the aging process as well. Chronic sleep deprivation has been linked to oxidative stress, inflammation, and cellular damage, which can contribute to the aging process. On the other hand, getting adequate sleep has been shown to have anti-aging effects, helping to slow down the rate of aging.

The Role of Exercise in the Aging Process: Exercise has been shown to have a range of anti-aging effects, including reducing oxidative stress, inflammation, and cellular damage, as well as promoting healthy mitochondrial function and hormone levels. Regular exercise can also help to slow down the rate of aging, as well as improving overall health and well-being.

The Impact of Nutrition on the Aging Process: Nutrition plays a crucial role in the aging process, as it provides the building blocks for cellular and tissue repair, as well as the energy needed for cellular function. A balanced diet that is rich in antioxidants, essential fatty acids, and other nutrients can help to slow down the rate of aging, as well as reducing the risk of age-related diseases.

The Effect of Social Engagement on the Aging Process: Social engagement and a sense of purpose are important factors in maintaining health and well-being as we age. Research has shown that social isolation and loneliness can increase the risk of age-related diseases, while social engagement and a sense of purpose can have anti-aging effects by reducing oxidative stress, inflammation, and cellular damage.

The Importance of Stress Management in the Aging Process: Chronic stress has been linked to oxidative stress, inflammation, and cellular damage, which can contribute to the aging process. On the other hand, stress management techniques such as mindfulness meditation, exercise, and relaxation can have anti-aging effects by reducing oxidative stress, inflammation, and cellular damage.

The Connection Between Chronic Disease and the Aging Process: Chronic diseases such as heart disease, diabetes, and cancer can have a major impact on the aging process, as they increase oxidative stress, inflammation, and cellular damage. Effective management of these diseases can help to slow down the rate of aging and improve overall health and well-being.

The Future of Anti-Aging Research: Anti-aging research is a rapidly evolving field, with new discoveries being made every year. Advances in the understanding of the underlying mechanisms of the aging process are helping to inform new strategies for slowing down the rate of aging and improving health outcomes for individuals as they age. These strategies include the use of anti-aging supplements, lifestyle modifications, and other interventions designed to reduce oxidative stress, inflammation, and cellular damage.

The Role of Telomeres in the Aging Process: Telomeres are the protective caps on the ends of our chromosomes, and they play a critical role in the aging process. As cells divide and telomeres become shorter, they can no longer provide protection to the chromosomes, leading to cellular damage and aging. Strategies such as reducing oxidative stress, improving mitochondrial function, and maintaining a healthy lifestyle can help to slow down the rate of telomere shortening and preserve healthy aging.

The Interplay Between Genetics and the Environment in the Aging Process: Both genetics and the environment play a role in the aging process. While some individuals may be genetically predisposed to age faster or slower, the environment and lifestyle factors can have a major impact on how quickly we age. By understanding the interplay between genetics and the environment, we can develop strategies for slowing down the rate of aging and improving overall health and well-being.

Conclusion:

In conclusion, time plays a crucial role in the aging process of living organisms, and this process is influenced by a complex interplay of factors including genetics, environmental factors, free radicals, and inflammation. Understanding the ways in which time affects the aging process is important for developing strategies to slow down the rate of aging and improve health outcomes for individuals as they age. Further research is needed to better understand the underlying mechanisms of the aging process, and to develop new interventions to improve the quality of life for older adults.

CHAPTER THREE

Is time a physical entity or a human construct?

Introduction:

The concept of time is one of the most fundamental and yet complex aspects of our universe. From the ancient Greeks to modern scientists, time has been a topic of philosophical and scientific inquiry for centuries. While time is a familiar aspect of our daily lives, the question of whether time is a physical entity or a human construct remains a subject of debate.

Body:

Time as a Physical Entity: From a physical perspective, time is often viewed as a dimension in which events occur in a linear and irreversible manner. According to this view, time is considered to be a physical entity that can be measured, quantified, and studied as a scientific phenomenon.

Time as a Human Construct. On the other hand, there are philosophical and psychological perspectives that argue that time is a human construct, rather than a physical entity. This view argues that our experience of time is shaped by our perceptions, memories, and other mental processes, and that time is a product of human consciousness and interpretation.

The Relativity of Time: One of the key arguments in favor of time being a human construct is the theory of relativity, which showed that time is relative and dependent on the observer's perspective. According to the theory of relativity, time can be distorted by gravity and other factors, and it is not a universal constant that applies to all observers equally.

The Concept of Time Dilation: Another aspect of the theory of relativity that supports the view of time as a human construct is the concept of time dilation. This concept refers to the observation that time appears to move at different rates for different observers, depending on their relative velocity and proximity to massive objects.

The Role of Consciousness in Perceiving Time: The argument that time is a human construct is further supported by the role of consciousness in perceiving time. Our experience of time is shaped by our mental processes, and our perception of time can be influenced by psychological factors such as attention, memory, and expectations.

Time and Causality: The relationship between time and causality is another aspect that contributes to the debate on whether time is a physical entity or a human construct. Some argue that time is a necessary condition for causality, while others argue that causality is independent of time. This relationship between time and causality has implications for our understanding of causality, as well as our understanding of time.

Time and Thermodynamics: The laws of thermodynamics also play a role in the debate on whether time is a physical entity or a human construct. The second law of thermodynamics, which states that entropy always increases over time, is often used to argue that time is a physical entity that can be quantified and studied scientifically.

Time and the Arrow of Time: The arrow of time is a concept that refers to the direction in which time is perceived to move. From a physical perspective, the arrow of time is often associated with the second law of thermodynamics and the increase in entropy over time. However, some argue that the arrow of time is a human construct, shaped by our mental processes and the way we perceive and experience time.

Time and the Quantum World: The study of quantum mechanics has also provided new insights into the nature of time. In the quantum world, time does not behave in the same way as it does in our classical experience of time. This has led some to argue that time is a human construct, shaped by our classical experience and our understanding of time in the classical world.

Time and the Multiverse: The concept of the multiverse, or the idea that there may be multiple universes with different physical properties and laws, also contributes to the debate on whether time is a physical entity or a human construct. Some argue that time is a physical entity that exists independently of our universe, while others argue that time is a human construct that is specific to our universe.

Time and the Human Experience: Finally, the human experience of time is another aspect that contributes to the debate on whether time is a physical entity or a human construct. Our experience of time is shaped by a variety of factors, including our mental processes, our emotions, and our cultural and societal influences. Understanding the human experience of time is critical for understanding the nature of time and its role in our lives.

Time and Relativity: The theory of relativity, first introduced by

Albert Einstein, has had a profound impact on our understanding of time. According to the theory of relativity, the perception of time is relative to the observer and is affected by the observer's velocity and proximity to a gravitational field. This has led some to argue that time is not a universal entity but rather a property of the observer.

Time and the Fabric of Space-Time: The concept of space-time as a four-dimensional fabric that describes the universe is central to modern physics. This view of space-time as a single entity has led some to argue that time is an inherent part of space-time and therefore a physical entity. Others argue that time is a human construct that emerges from our perception of the universe.

Time and Consciousness: The role of consciousness in shaping our perception of time is also a topic of debate. Some argue that consciousness creates the experience of time, while others argue that time exists independently of consciousness. This is a particularly important question in the context of time travel, as it has implications for our understanding of the nature of time and its relationship to consciousness.

Time and Philosophy: Philosophers have also been interested in the nature of time for centuries. The concept of time has been discussed in various philosophical traditions, including metaphysics, epistemology, and ethics.

These discussions have contributed to our understanding of time and its relationship to reality and have provided different perspectives on whether time is a physical entity or a human construct.

Time and Science: The scientific study of time has been a central focus of research for centuries. This includes the development of theories and models that describe the behavior of time, as well as empirical studies that test these theories. The study of time is a complex and interdisciplinary field that draws on many different areas of science, including physics, biology, psychology, and neuroscience.

Time and Culture: Our cultural and societal views of time also play a role in shaping our understanding of time. Different cultures and societies have different views on the nature of time and its role in our lives, and these views can have a profound impact on how we experience and understand time. Understanding the cultural and societal views of time is critical for a comprehensive understanding of time and its role in our lives.

The Arrow of Time: One of the key characteristics of time is the concept of the arrow of time, which refers to the idea that time flows in a particular direction. This is often described as a "one-way" flow, from the

past to the future, and is associated with the concept of entropy and the second law of thermodynamics. The arrow of time is a crucial aspect of our understanding of time, as it gives us a sense of direction and progression in time.

Time in Quantum Mechanics: The concept of time in quantum mechanics is a topic of much debate and disagreement. Some interpretations of quantum mechanics suggest that time is a fundamental aspect of the universe, while others argue that time is an emergent property that arises from the interactions of quantum particles. This is a complex and ongoing area of research that has important implications for our understanding of the nature of time and the relationship between quantum mechanics and general relativity.

The Paradoxes of Time Travel: The possibility of time travel raises a number of paradoxes and ethical considerations. For example, the grandfather paradox asks whether it is possible to travel back in time and kill your own grandfather, which would result in a paradox as it would mean that you would never have been born. Other paradoxes, such as the predestination paradox, raise questions about the role of free will and determinism in the context of time travel.

The Experience of Time: The experience of time is also a topic of interest. Research has shown that the experience of time is subjective and can be influenced by factors such as attention, emotion, and memory. These findings have important implications for our understanding of time and its relationship to perception and consciousness.

The Future of Time: The study of time is a rapidly advancing field with new developments and discoveries being made all the time. From the development of new technologies for measuring time to the exploration of new theories and models, the future of time research is exciting and full of possibilities. The continuing study of time will help us to gain a deeper understanding of this fundamental aspect of our universe and our lives.

The Relationship between Time and Space: Another important aspect of time is its relationship to space. The concept of spacetime, first proposed by Albert Einstein, describes the idea that space and time are not separate entities, but are instead intertwined and form a single four-dimensional fabric. This view of spacetime has been supported by numerous experiments and observations and has had a profound impact on our understanding of physics and cosmology.

The Nature of Time in Relativity: In Einstein's theory of relativity, time is not a constant and unchanging entity, but is instead relative to the observer and depends on the observer's velocity and position in space. This leads to the well-known effects of time dilation and length contraction, which have been confirmed by numerous experiments and observations.

Time and the Nature of Reality: The nature of time and its relationship to reality is a topic of much debate and speculation. Some philosophers argue that time is an illusion and that

reality exists only in the present moment, while others see time as a fundamental aspect of the universe that influences the way things exist and change. The debate over the nature of time has important implications for our understanding of the world and the nature of reality itself.

Time and the Human Mind: The human mind plays a crucial role in our experience of time. Our perception of time is shaped by our memories, emotions, and expectations, and can be influenced by factors such as attention, stress, and boredom. This has important implications for our understanding of the subjective experience of time and the relationship between the mind and time.

Time and the Brain: The study of time and its relationship to the brain is a rapidly advancing field. Research has shown that different areas of the brain are involved in different aspects of time perception, such as estimating duration, maintaining attention, and processing events in a temporal order. These findings have important implications for our understanding of the neural mechanisms underlying time perception and the relationship between the brain and time.

Time and Culture: The concept of time is also shaped by cultural and historical factors. Different cultures and historical periods have different ways of measuring and experiencing time, and these can have a profound impact on the way people think about and understand time. Understanding the cultural and historical context of time can help us to gain a deeper appreciation of its role in human life and culture.

Conclusion: Time is a complex and multifaceted concept that has been studied by scientists, philosophers, and theologians for centuries. Despite our best efforts, the true nature of time remains elusive and many questions about time remain unanswered. However, the ongoing study of time will help us to gain a deeper understanding of this fundamental aspect of the universe and our lives.

Conclusion:

In conclusion, the question of whether time is a physical entity or a human construct remains a subject of debate. While the physical view of time as a dimension in which events occur in a linear and irreversible manner is widely accepted, the philosophical and psychological perspectives that argue that time is a human construct are also compelling. Ultimately, the answer to this question may depend on the perspective of the observer and the context in which time is being considered. Regardless of whether time is considered to be a physical entity or a human construct, it remains a fundamental and intriguing aspect of our universe that will continue to be a subject of scientific and philosophical inquiry for years to come.

CHAPTER FOUR

How does gravity influence the passage of time?

Introduction:

Gravity is one of the fundamental forces of nature that has a profound influence on the universe. It affects everything from the motion of celestial bodies to the behavior of light and other forms of energy. In this chapter, we will explore the relationship between gravity and the passage of time, and how gravity influences the way we experience and measure time.

Body Content:

The Theory of General Relativity: The connection between gravity and the passage of time is described by Albert Einstein's theory of general relativity, which provides a comprehensive description of the behavior of gravity. In this theory, gravity is not a force between masses, but rather a curvature of spacetime caused by the presence of mass.

The Effects of Gravity on Time Dilation: One of the most important effects of gravity on time is time dilation, which refers to the stretching or slowing of time in a gravitational field. According to general relativity, time runs slower near massive objects, and the stronger the gravitational field, the more time is slowed.

The GPS and Time Dilation: One of the most striking examples of the influence of gravity on time is the Global Positioning System (GPS), which relies on precise measurements of time to provide navigation information. The GPS system must take into account the effects of time dilation due to the Earth's gravity, as well as the gravitational pull of the sun and moon, in order to provide accurate navigation information.

The Influence of Gravity on Clocks: Clocks that are at different elevations in a gravitational field will run at different rates, due to the influence of gravity on time. This has important implications for the design of clocks and timing systems that are used for scientific and engineering applications.

The Connection between Gravity and Black Holes: One of the most extreme effects of gravity on time can be seen in the case of black holes, which are regions of spacetime where gravity is so strong that it distorts time and space to the point where not even light can escape. According to general relativity, time slows down near a black hole and comes to a complete stop at the black hole's event horizon.

The Search for Gravitational Waves: The study of gravitational waves, which are ripples in spacetime caused by the acceleration of massive objects, provides a powerful tool for exploring the relationship between gravity and the passage of time. By studying gravitational waves, scientists are able to learn about the behavior of gravity and the structure of the universe in ways that were previously not possible.

The Gravitational Redshift: Another important effect of gravity on time is the gravitational redshift, which refers to the shift in frequency of light or other forms of electromagnetic radiation that are emitted in a gravitational field. This effect is a result of the stretching of spacetime in a gravitational field, and provides a direct measurement of the influence of gravity on the passage of time.

The Twin Paradox: The twin paradox is a thought experiment that demonstrates the influence of gravity on the passage of time in a moving reference frame. In this experiment, two twins are separated, with one twin remaining on Earth and the other traveling at a high speed in a spaceship. Upon the return of the traveling twin, it is found that time has passed differently for each twin due to the different gravitational influences experienced by each.

The Role of Gravity in the Expansion of the Universe: The expansion of the universe is another example of the connection between gravity and time. According to current theories of cosmology, the expansion of the universe is driven by dark energy, a mysterious form of energy that is causing the universe to expand at an accelerating rate. However, gravity also plays a role in the expansion of the universe by slowing down the rate of expansion in certain regions and causing the formation of structure such as galaxies and clusters of galaxies.

The Quest for a Unified Theory of Gravity and Quantum Mechanics: One of the greatest challenges facing scientists today is the quest for a unified theory of gravity and quantum mechanics. While general relativity provides a comprehensive description of the behavior of gravity on large scales, quantum mechanics provides a different and complementary description of the behavior of matter and energy on small scales. A successful unification of these two theories would provide a more complete understanding of the relationship between gravity and the passage of time, and could lead to new technologies and advancements in our understanding of the universe.

The Study of Gravity Waves: The study of gravity waves provides a unique window into the behavior of gravity and its influence on time. By observing the interactions between massive objects and the ripples in spacetime that they create, scientists are able to learn about the behavior of gravity in extreme environments, such as near black holes and in the aftermath of the Big Bang.

The Role of Gravity in the Formation and Evolution of Galaxies: The influence of gravity on the passage of time also plays a critical role in the formation and evolution of galaxies. The gravitational forces between massive objects, such as stars and black holes, determine the motion of these objects and the distribution of matter within a galaxy. The study of gravity and its effects on time therefore provides important insights into the structure and evolution of the universe.

The Role of Gravity in the Formation of Planetary Systems: In addition to its role in the formation and evolution of galaxies, gravity plays a critical role in the formation of planetary systems. The gravitational forces between a star and its surrounding planets determine the stability and orbit of these planets, and the study of these interactions provides important information about the formation and evolution of planetary systems.

The Influence of Gravity on the Aging Process: The influence of gravity on the aging process is an area of ongoing research. While it is known that gravity affects the physiological processes of living organisms, it is still not clear how this influence impacts the aging process. Some studies have suggested that the presence of gravity may play a role in regulating cellular processes, and that changes in gravity can have a significant impact on the rate of aging.

The Importance of Gravity in Modern Technology: The study of gravity and its effects on time is critical to the development of modern technology. From GPS navigation systems to the study of black holes, a deep understanding of gravity is essential to many areas of research and technology. The ability to accurately measure and model the behavior of gravity is therefore crucial to the advancement of science and technology.

Conclusion: The relationship between gravity and time is a complex and multifaceted subject that continues to be the focus of ongoing research and investigation. From the influence of gravity on the aging process to its role in the formation and evolution of the universe, the study of gravity and its effects on time is critical to our understanding of the world around us. Through continued research and investigation, scientists and technology experts are working to deepen our understanding of the behavior of gravity and its impact on the passage of time, and to develop new and innovative technologies that can help us better understand this fascinating and important subject.

Gravitational Time Dilation: One of the most significant effects of gravity on the passage of time is gravitational time dilation. This phenomenon occurs when an object is subjected to a strong gravitational field, causing time to pass more slowly in the vicinity of the object than in regions of weaker gravity. This effect was first predicted by

Einstein's theory of general relativity and has since been confirmed through numerous experiments and observations.

Black Holes and Gravitational Time Dilation: Black holes are objects with extremely strong gravitational fields, and as a result, they provide a unique opportunity to study the effects of gravity on time. Observations of black holes have shown that time passes much more slowly near the event horizon, the boundary beyond which not even light can escape. This provides a dramatic example of the effects of gravity on the passage of time and highlights the importance of continued study in this area.

The Interplay between Gravity and Quantum Mechanics: Another important area of research in the relationship between gravity and time is the interplay between these two physical phenomena and the implications this has for our understanding of the universe. Despite their fundamental differences, gravity and quantum mechanics are thought to be intimately linked, and the study of this interplay is critical to our understanding of the behavior of the universe at its smallest scales.

The Importance of Precision Measurements: Precision measurements are critical in the study of the relationship between gravity and time. The ability to make accurate and precise measurements of gravity and time is essential to understanding the underlying physical processes involved, and to developing new theories and models that can help us better understand the world around us. The use of advanced technologies such as atom interferometry and satellite-based gravimeters is playing a critical role in this area of research.

Future Directions in the Study of Gravity and Time: As our understanding of gravity and time continues to evolve, new and exciting research directions are emerging. From the search for gravitational waves and the study of black holes to the development of new technologies for precision measurements, the future of research in this area is filled with exciting possibilities. Through continued exploration and investigation, scientists and technology experts are working to deepen our understanding of the relationship between gravity and time and to advance our knowledge of the world around us.

The Implications of Gravity on Time for Astrophysics and Astronomy: Understanding the relationship between gravity and time has significant implications for the study of astronomy and astrophysics. For example, by studying the effects of gravity on time, scientists are able to better understand the behavior of objects such as black holes and neutron stars. This information is critical in our understanding of the evolution of stars and the formation of galaxies.

The Role of Time in the Study of Relativity: The relationship between gravity and time is also critical to our understanding of the theory of relativity. By studying the effects of gravity on time, scientists are able to better understand the behavior of objects in motion and the implications of this motion for our understanding of the universe. This includes the effects of gravity on light and the way in which gravity affects the passage of time, providing new insights into the behavior of the universe at both large and small scales.

The Importance of Time for Cosmology and the Big Bang Theory: In the field of cosmology, the study of the relationship between gravity and time is critical in our understanding of the early universe and the formation of structures such as galaxies and stars. By understanding the behavior of time in the early universe, scientists are able to gain new insights into the Big Bang theory and the evolution of the universe.

The Relationship between Time and Space: The relationship between time and space is another important area of research in the field of physics. Scientists are exploring the ways in which time and space are interconnected and the implications this has for our understanding of the universe. This includes the study of the behavior of objects in motion, the effects of gravity on time, and the implications of time dilation.

The Role of Time in the Search for a Grand Unifying Theory: The study of time and its relationship with other physical phenomena is also critical in the search for a grand unifying theory. This theory aims to provide a complete and coherent explanation of the physical world, and includes our understanding of the relationship between gravity and time. The ongoing investigation into this relationship will play a critical role in advancing our understanding of the universe and the laws that govern its behavior.

Time Dilation and the Theory of Relativity: Time dilation, which refers to the phenomenon of time moving at different rates for objects in different states of motion or in different gravitational fields, is a direct consequence of the theory of relativity. This theory states that the laws of physics are the same for all observers, regardless of their relative velocity or their position within a gravitational field. Time dilation is a fundamental prediction of the theory of relativity and has been confirmed by numerous experiments.

The Concept of Time and the Nature of Reality: The nature of time is a long-standing philosophical question that has been explored by scholars and scientists for centuries. Some argue that time is a fundamental aspect of the universe, while others see it as a human construct that is used to describe and understand the physical world. Regardless of one's perspective, it is clear that time plays a critical role in our understanding of reality and the behavior of the physical world.

The Implications of Time for our Understanding of Consciousness: The relationship between time and consciousness is another area of research that has garnered much interest in recent years. Scientists are exploring the ways in which our perception of time is linked to our experience of consciousness and how this relationship might impact our understanding of the nature of consciousness itself.

The Role of Time in the Study of Quantum Mechanics: The study of time also has important implications for our understanding of quantum mechanics. This theory describes the behavior of matter and energy at the smallest scales, and raises important questions about the nature of time and its relationship to the physical world. Scientists are exploring these questions in the hopes of gaining a deeper understanding of quantum mechanics and its implications for our understanding of the universe.

The Importance of Time for the Development of Technology: The study of time and its relationship with other physical phenomena has practical applications in the development of technology. For example, the study of time dilation has implications for the design of GPS satellites, which must account for the effects of time dilation in order to provide accurate navigation information. Additionally, the study of time and its relationship to the physical world is critical in the development of new technologies, such as quantum computers, which rely on a deep understanding of time and its behavior.

Conclusion:

Gravity has a profound influence on the passage of time, and this relationship is a central aspect of our understanding of the universe. From the effects of time dilation near massive objects to the behavior of black holes and the search for gravitational waves, the study of gravity and time continues to provide new insights into the nature of the universe and our place within it.

CHAPTER FIVE

How can a person manipulate their perception of time to make it seem faster or slower?

Introduction

The perception of time is subjective and varies from person to person. It can change based on different circumstances and events, such as boredom, excitement, stress, or anticipation. However, there is evidence to suggest that a person can manipulate their perception of time to make it seem faster or slower. In this Chpater, we will explore the various methods that a person can use to control their perception of time.

Perception of Time and the Brain

The perception of time is a complex cognitive process that is processed in various regions of the brain. The brain creates an internal representation of time based on sensory information, memories, and expectations. The perception of time is not an objective measure of the passage of time, but rather a subjective interpretation.

Methods to Make Time Seem Faster or Slower

There are several methods that a person can use to manipulate their perception of time, making it seem faster or slower. These methods include the following:

Attention

The brain processes information faster when it is attentive, which can cause time to appear to move more quickly. This is why time seems to fly by when you are focused on a task that you enjoy or when you are in a state of flow. On the other hand, time seems to drag when you are bored, distracted, or uninterested.

Anticipation

Anticipation can also have an impact on the perception of time. When a person is eagerly awaiting an event, such as a vacation or a special occasion, time seems to move more slowly. However, once the event has arrived, time seems to speed up.

Memories

Memories can also play a role in the perception of time. When a person has positive memories of an event, they tend to think of it as being shorter than it was. On the other hand, when a person has negative memories of an event, they tend to think of it as being longer than it was.

Stress

Stress and anxiety can cause time to appear to move more slowly. When a person is stressed, they are often in a state of high alert, which causes the brain to process information more slowly. This can make time seem to drag.

Mindfulness

Mindfulness is a state of awareness that is achieved by focusing on the present moment. When a person is mindful, they are more aware of the present moment, which can cause time to appear to move more slowly. This is because mindfulness allows a person to fully experience and process each moment.

Perception of Time and Emotions

Emotions also play a role in the perception of time. Positive emotions, such as happiness, joy, and excitement, tend to make time seem to move more quickly. This is because the brain processes positive emotions more quickly and with less effort, allowing time to appear to move more quickly. On the other hand, negative emotions, such as sadness, anger, and fear, tend to make time seem to move more slowly. This is because negative emotions require more effort to process, which can cause time to appear to drag.

Perception of Time and Attentional Blink

The attentional blink is a phenomenon that occurs when a person is unable to process information quickly enough. This can cause time to appear to move more slowly because the person is unable to process the events happening around them. The attentional blink can be caused by a variety of factors, including stress, anxiety, and fatigue.

Perception of Time and Age

Age can also have an impact on the perception of time. As a person ages, their perception of time can change. This is because the brain's ability to process information changes as a person ages, which can cause time to appear to move more slowly. Additionally, older people often have more experiences and memories to draw from, which can cause time to appear to move more quickly.

Perception of Time and Sleep

Sleep can also have an impact on the perception of time. When a person is well-rested, their brain processes information more quickly, which can cause time to appear to move more quickly. On the other hand, when a person is tired, their brain processes information more slowly, which can cause time to appear to move more slowly.

Perception of Time and Mental Health

Mental health can also have an impact on the perception of time. People with mental health conditions, such as depression and anxiety, often experience a distorted perception of time. This can cause time to appear to move more slowly or more quickly, depending on the individual and their condition.

Perception of Time and Attention

Attention is a crucial factor in the perception of time. When a person is fully focused and attentive, time seems to move more quickly. On the other hand, when a person is distracted or uninterested, time seems to drag. For example, when a person is engaged in an enjoyable activity, such as playing a sport, watching a movie, or reading a book, time seems to fly by. In contrast, when a person is performing a tedious task, such as filling out paperwork or waiting in line, time seems to move much more slowly.

Perception of Time and Mindset

The mindset a person adopts can also impact the perception of time. A person who has a growth mindset, which involves viewing challenges and obstacles as opportunities for growth and development, tends to experience time as passing more quickly. On the other hand, a person who has a fixed mindset, which involves viewing challenges and obstacles as insurmountable and unchanging, tends to experience time as passing more slowly.

Perception of Time and Movement

Movement can also impact the perception of time. When a person is in motion, such as running, riding a bike, or driving a car, time seems to move more quickly. On the other hand, when a person is stationary, such as sitting in a chair or standing in line, time seems to move more slowly. This is because movement provides a sense of progress and forward momentum, which can cause time to appear to move more quickly.

Perception of Time and Sensory Stimulation

Sensory stimulation can also impact the perception of time. When a person is surrounded by intense sensory stimulation, such as bright lights, loud music, or fast-moving images, time seems to move more quickly. On the other hand, when a person is surrounded by limited sensory stimulation, such as a quiet room or a calm environment, time seems to move more slowly.

Perception of Time and Social Connection

Social connection can also impact the perception of time. When a person is surrounded by friends, family, or other people, time seems to move more quickly. This is because social connections provide a sense of enjoyment and fulfillment, which can cause time to appear to move more quickly. On the other hand, when a person is isolated or alone, time seems to move more slowly.

Perception of Time and Music

Music also plays a role in the perception of time. Certain types of music, such as fast-paced music with a strong beat, can cause time to seem to move more quickly. This is because the music provides a sense of rhythm and momentum, which can make time appear to move more quickly. On the other hand, slower and more relaxing music can cause time to seem to move more slowly. This is because the music creates a sense of calm and tranquility, which can make time appear to move more slowly.

Perception of Time and Environment

The environment in which a person is located can also impact their perception of time. A cluttered or distracting environment can cause time to seem to move more slowly, while a calm and organized environment can cause time to seem to move more quickly. This is because a cluttered or distracting environment can cause a person to become distracted and disorganized, while a calm and organized environment can help a person to focus and be more productive.

Perception of Time and Expectations

Expectations can also impact the perception of time. When a person has high expectations for an event or situation, time seems to move more slowly. This is because the person is eagerly anticipating the event, which can cause time to appear to drag. On the other hand, when a person has low expectations for an event or situation, time seems to move more quickly. This is because the person is not as invested in the event, which can cause time to appear to move more quickly.

Perception of Time and Stress

Stress can also impact the perception of time. When a person is stressed, time seems to move more slowly. This is because stress causes a person to become more focused and aware of their surroundings, which can make time appear to move more slowly. On the other hand, when a person is relaxed, time seems to move more quickly. This is because relaxation allows a person to be more relaxed and less focused on their surroundings, which can make time appear to move more quickly.

Perception of Time and Physical Movement

Physical movement can also impact the perception of time. When a person is engaged in physical activity, such as running or dancing, time seems to move more quickly. This is because the physical movement provides a sense of momentum and energy, which can make time appear to move more quickly. On the other hand, when a person is sitting or lying down, time seems to move more slowly. This is because the lack of movement can make time appear to move more slowly.

Perception of Time and Attention

Attention is another factor that can impact the perception of time. When a person is focused on a task or activity, time seems to move more quickly. This is because the person is fully engaged and absorbed in the task, which can make time appear to move more quickly. On the other hand, when a person is bored or distracted, time seems to move more slowly. This is because the person is not fully engaged or invested in the task, which can make time appear to move more slowly.

Perception of Time and Sensory Stimulation

Sensory stimulation can also impact the perception of time. When a person is exposed to a high level of sensory stimulation, such as bright lights or loud noises, time seems to move more quickly. This is because the high level of stimulation can cause a person to become more focused and alert, which can make time appear to move more quickly. On the other hand, when a person is exposed to a low level of sensory stimulation, such as a calm and quiet environment, time seems to move more slowly. This is because the low level of stimulation can cause a person to become more relaxed and calm, which can make time appear to move more slowly.

Perception of Time and Social Connection

Finally, social connection can also impact the perception of time. When a person is engaged in social activities, such as talking with friends or family, time seems to move more quickly. This is because the social interaction provides a sense of energy and excitement, which can make time appear to move more quickly. On the other hand, when a person is isolated or lonely, time seems to move more slowly. This is because the lack of social interaction can cause a person to become more introspective and focused on their thoughts, which can make time appear to move more slowly.

Perception of Time and Emotions

Emotions also play a crucial role in the perception of time. Research has shown that people tend to perceive time as moving more slowly during negative emotions such as anxiety or fear, and more quickly during positive emotions like happiness and excitement. This is because emotions can change the focus of attention, and can influence the perception of time by making it feel longer or shorter. For example, when a person is feeling anxious or stressed, their focus may be on their thoughts or worries, causing them to experience time as moving more slowly. On the other hand, when a person is feeling happy and excited, their focus may be on the present moment and the sensations they are experiencing, causing time to move more quickly.

Perception of Time and Expectations

Expectations can also impact the perception of time. People tend to perceive time as moving more quickly when they have a clear idea of what is going to happen next, or when they are focused on a specific goal. This is because having a clear idea of what is going to happen can help to focus attention and create a sense of momentum, making time feel like it is moving more quickly. On the other hand, when a person lacks clarity about what is going to happen next, or when they are uncertain about the future, time can seem to move more slowly. This is because uncertainty can lead to a lack of focus and can create a sense of boredom, making time feel like it is dragging on.

Perception of Time and Mindfulness

Finally, mindfulness can also impact the perception of time. Mindfulness involves being present and focused on the present moment, and can help people to experience time as moving more quickly. This is because mindfulness can help to reduce distractions, increase focus and engagement, and create a sense of connection with the present moment. This can help people to experience time as moving more quickly and to feel more in control of their experience. On the other hand, when people are not mindful and are easily distracted, time can seem to move more slowly. This is because distractions can disrupt focus and can create a sense of boredom or disconnectedness, making time feel like it is dragging on.

Perception of Time and Attention

Attention is a critical factor that affects the perception of time. The way in which a person directs their attention can influence the perception of time, making it feel faster or slower. For instance, when a person is focused on a particular task, they tend to experience time as moving more quickly as their attention is directed towards the task and they are not easily distracted. On the other hand, when a person is distracted and their attention is not focused, they tend to experience time as moving more slowly. This can be seen in activities such as waiting in line or being stuck in traffic, where the lack of focus can make time seem to drag on.

Perception of Time and Memory

Memory also plays a crucial role in the perception of time. People tend to remember events that are rich in sensory details, such as sights, sounds, and emotions, as lasting longer than events that are less memorable. This is because these sensory details tend to increase the focus and attention, leading to a more vivid memory that can stretch the perception of time. For example, a person who is attending a concert may remember the experience as lasting longer than it actually did because of the rich sensory experience and the focus on the music and performers.

Perception of Time and Age

Age can also influence the perception of time. Research has shown that as people get older, they tend to perceive time as moving more quickly. This is because older people often have a greater perspective on time and a longer life span, which can make time seem to be moving more quickly. On the other hand, children tend to perceive time as moving more slowly because they have a shorter life span and a limited perspective on time.

Perception of Time and Music

Music is another factor that can affect the perception of time. Research has shown that listening to music can alter the perception of time, making it feel longer or shorter depending on the tempo and rhythm of the music. For example, slow-paced music can make time seem to move more slowly, while fast-paced music can make time seem to move more quickly. This is because music has a direct impact on our emotions and state of mind, which can shape the perception of time.

In conclusion, the perception of time is complex and influenced by a variety of factors such as attention, memory, age, music, and more. By understanding these factors, people can gain greater control over their perception of time and make it feel faster or slower depending on their needs and goals. Whether it is through attention, memory, music, or other strategies, people can enhance their experience of time and improve their well-being, quality of life, and overall enjoyment of life.

CHAPTER SIX

Can memories and experiences be stored in time, and retrieved later?

Introduction: The question of whether memories and experiences can be stored in time and retrieved later is a complex and multi-disciplinary one that has attracted interest from scientists, philosophers, and psychologists alike. This chapter will explore the current state of research on this topic and the different perspectives that have been proposed.

Body:

The Neuroscientific Perspective: From a neuroscientific perspective, memories and experiences are thought to be stored in the brain as patterns of neural activity. This idea is supported by numerous studies that have shown that the brain's activity patterns change in response to experiences, and that these changes can be used to reconstruct memories.

The Psychological Perspective: Psychologists have proposed several theories to explain how memories and experiences are stored and retrieved. Some of these theories focus on the role of attention and encoding, while others propose that memories are stored in a hierarchical manner and retrieved based on their contextual associations.

The Philosophical Perspective: Philosophers have explored the relationship between memories and experiences and the concept of time. Some argue that memories and experiences exist in a timeless realm, while others propose that they are inherently tied to our perception of time.

The Concept of Time and Memory: The relationship between time and memory is complex and multi-faceted. Some researchers propose that time is an essential aspect of memory and that it is used to organize and categorize memories, while others argue that time is a human construct that is imposed on memories after they have been formed.

The Implications of Time for Memory Retrieval: The role of time in memory retrieval is a critical area of research. Some researchers propose that memories are stored in a temporal context and that this context influences their retrieval, while others argue that memories are retrieved based on their content and associations.

The Role of Emotion in Memory Retrieval: Emotion is another factor that has been shown to play a critical role in memory retrieval. Research has shown that memories that are associated with strong emotions are more likely to be remembered, and that these memories can be retrieved more easily than memories that are not associated with strong emotions.

The Use of Technology to Store and Retrieve Memories: Advances in technology have also led to the development of new tools and techniques for storing and retrieving memories. For example, the development of brain-computer interfaces has the potential to allow us to store and retrieve memories in a more direct and efficient manner.

The Role of Age in Memory Retrieval: Age is another factor that influences the retrieval of memories. As individuals age, they are more likely to experience memory decline, and the speed and accuracy of their memory retrieval may decline as well. Some researchers propose that this decline is due to changes in the brain's structure and function, while others argue that it is due to changes in the way that memories are encoded and retrieved.

The Relationship between Time and False Memories: Another area of interest is the relationship between time and the formation of false memories. Research has shown that time can influence the accuracy of memories, and that false memories are more likely to be formed as the time between the original event and the time of recall increases.

The Role of Time in Memory Consolidation: Memory consolidation is the process by which newly formed memories are stabilized and become permanent. Research has shown that time is an important factor in the consolidation of memories, and that the passage of time can facilitate the formation of new, more stable memories.

The Potential for Time Travel and Memory Retrieval: The concept of time travel has also raised questions about the possibility of storing and retrieving memories from different points in time. Some researchers propose that time travel could allow us to access memories and experiences from the past, while others argue that it is unlikely to be possible due to the complex and interrelated nature of time and memory.

The Role of Sleep in Memory Consolidation: Sleep is another important factor that can influence memory consolidation and retrieval. Research has shown that sleep can improve the consolidation of memories and help to strengthen the neural connections that support memory storage. Additionally, sleep can play a role in enhancing the retrieval of memories, particularly in the case of declarative memories, which are memories that can be consciously recalled.

The Importance of Emotion in Memory Retrieval: Emotion also plays a significant role in memory retrieval. Research has shown that memories that are associated with strong emotions are more likely to be remembered and retrieved than memories that are not associated with emotion. This is because emotions are thought to create stronger neural connections in the brain that support memory storage and retrieval.

The Influence of Context on Memory Retrieval: Context is another important factor that can influence memory retrieval. Research has shown that the context in which a memory was formed can play a significant role in the retrieval of that memory. This is because the context can provide cues that can trigger the recall of associated memories, making it easier to retrieve those memories.

The Effect of Cognitive Processes on Memory Retrieval: Finally, cognitive processes can play a significant role in memory retrieval. Research has shown that the type of mental processing that an individual engages in during the formation of a memory can influence the likelihood of that memory being retrieved later. For example, elaborative encoding, which involves creating a rich and detailed mental representation of a memory, has been shown to enhance memory retrieval.

The Role of Brain Structures in Memory Retrieval: The brain contains various structures that play a role in memory retrieval, including the hippocampus, the amygdala, and the neocortex. The hippocampus is considered to be a key structure for the formation and retrieval of declarative memories, while the amygdala plays a role in the processing of emotional memories. The neocortex is also thought to play a role in memory retrieval, as it is responsible for higher-level processing of information and is involved in the consolidation of long-term memories.

The Relationship between Memory and Reality: The relationship between memory and reality is a complex and controversial topic that has been the subject of much debate. Some researchers argue that memories are a veridical representation of past experiences, while others suggest that memories are inherently flawed and that their accuracy can be influenced by a number of factors. This debate has important implications for our understanding of the nature of memory and the role it plays in shaping our perceptions of reality.

The Potential for Memory Manipulation: The potential for memory manipulation is another important issue that has emerged in recent years, particularly with the advancement of technologies such as brain-computer interfaces. The ability to manipulate memories raises important ethical and moral considerations, as well as concerns about the accuracy and reliability of memories.

The Role of Culture in Memory Retrieval: Culture can also play a role in memory retrieval. Research has shown that cultural differences can influence the way that individuals process and store memories, as well as the types of memories that are remembered and retrieved. For example, cultural differences can influence the importance of social, emotional, and contextual information in memory retrieval.

Advances in Memory Research: Advances in memory research have the potential to provide new insights into the mechanisms of memory retrieval and the role that various factors play in this process. For example, the development of brain imaging technologies, such as fMRI, has provided researchers with a new tool for investigating the neural processes that underlie memory retrieval. Additionally, advances in the fields of neuroscience, psychology, and computer science have the potential to revolutionize our understanding of memory and its role in shaping our experiences and perceptions of reality.

However, there is still much debate and research being conducted in the field of memory and its relationship with time. Some scientists argue that memories are stored in specific brain regions, and that their retrieval is dependent on the stimulation of these regions through external cues or internal thoughts. Others believe that memories are stored in the synaptic connections between neurons, and that their recall is dependent on the reactivation of these connections.

Despite these different theories, it is widely agreed that memories are not static entities, but rather dynamic and malleable. They can be influenced by various factors, such as emotion, attention, and even aging. For example, when a person recalls a memory, they may change certain aspects of it to better fit their current perception or beliefs. This malleability of memories raises questions about their reliability and accuracy, as well as the possibility of their storage in time.

In conclusion, while there is still much to be learned about the nature of memories and their relationship with time, it is clear that they play a crucial role in shaping our understanding of the world and our place in it. Whether or not memories and experiences can be stored in time and retrieved later remains an open question, but one that will likely continue to be explored by scientists and philosophers alike. Understanding the factors that influence memory retrieval has important implications for the development of memory-enhancing strategies and interventions, as well as for our understanding of the nature of memories and experiences. Ongoing research and advances in technology have the potential to revolutionize our understanding of memory and its role in shaping our perceptions of reality. While much is still unknown about the role that these factors play in memory retrieval, ongoing research and advances in technology have the potential to provide new insights and advancements in this field. Understanding the factors that influence memory retrieval has important implications for the development of memory-enhancing strategies and interventions, as well as for our understanding of the nature of memories and experiences.

CHAPTER SEVEN

What is the relationship between time and space, and how do they interact with each other?

Introduction

The relationship between time and space is one of the most fundamental questions in physics and philosophy. Time and space are two essential concepts that are intertwined and interact with each other in a variety of ways. The relationship between time and space is the basis of our understanding of the world and the laws of physics that govern it. This Chapter will examine the relationship between time and space, and how they interact with each other.

Theories of Time and Space

One of the earliest theories of time and space was proposed by Sir Isaac Newton in the 17th century. Newton believed that time and space were independent and absolute, meaning that they existed independently of each other and had their own separate properties. He viewed time as a continuous flow that was not affected by the events in space, and space as a fixed, three-dimensional framework in which all events occur.

In the 20th century, Albert Einstein challenged Newton's views with his theory of general relativity. Einstein argued that time and space are not independent and absolute, but rather they are interdependent and relative to the observer. He demonstrated that time is not a continuous flow, but is affected by the presence of mass and gravity. He also showed that space is not fixed and three-dimensional, but can be distorted by the presence of mass and gravity.

The Interaction between Time and Space

The interaction between time and space can be seen in a number of different phenomena, including the phenomenon of time dilation. Time dilation occurs when time passes more slowly in a strong gravitational field than it does in a weaker one. This phenomenon occurs because time is affected by the presence of mass and gravity, and is a direct result of the interaction between time and space.

Another example of the interaction between time and space is the phenomenon of black holes. Black holes are regions of space where the gravitational pull is so strong that not even light can escape. The intense gravitational field of a black hole distorts time and space in a way that causes time to pass more slowly for objects near the black hole. This is another demonstration of the interdependence of time and space and the way in which they interact with each other. Time and space are two essential concepts that are intertwined and interact with each other in a variety of ways. Newton's theory of time and space as independent and absolute was challenged by Einstein's theory of general relativity, which showed that time and space are interdependent and relative to the observer. The interaction between time and space can be seen in a number of different phenomena, including time dilation and black holes, demonstrating the interdependence and interaction of these two concepts.

One of the most significant implications of the interaction between time and space is the concept of spacetime. Spacetime is the combination of three-dimensional space and one-dimensional time into a single four-dimensional structure. This concept was first proposed by Hermann Minkowski, who was a student of Einstein. Minkowski argued that the combination of space and time into a single structure was necessary to fully understand the effects of mass and gravity on time and space.

The theory of spacetime has been used to explain many phenomena in physics, including the curvature of spacetime caused by the presence of mass and gravity. This curvature leads to the phenomenon of gravitational lensing, which is the bending of light by massive objects. It has also been used to explain the phenomenon of quantum entanglement, where particles are connected in such a way that their properties are correlated even when separated by large distances.

Another significant implication of the interaction between time and space is the concept of time travel. Time travel is the idea that it is possible to travel through time, either forwards or backwards. While time travel is still a purely theoretical concept, it is based on the idea that time and space are interdependent and can be affected by the presence of mass and gravity. The interaction between time and space has many significant implications for our understanding of the world. The concept of spacetime has been used to explain many phenomena in physics, including the curvature of spacetime and the phenomenon of gravitational lensing. The interaction between time and space has also given rise to the idea of time travel, which remains a purely theoretical concept. Nevertheless, the relationship between time and space continues to be one of the most fundamental questions in physics and philosophy, and the study of their interaction continues to play a central role in our understanding of the world.

Another aspect of the relationship between time and space is the concept of causality. Causality is the idea that events in the world have causes and effects, and that these events occur in a specific order in time. Causality is a fundamental principle of physics and is based on the idea that time and space are interconnected.

In physics, causality is a crucial concept in the study of the laws of motion. The laws of motion describe how objects move in space and time, and are based on the idea that cause and effect relationships determine the motion of objects. This means that the position and velocity of an object at any given time are determined by the forces acting on it and the previous positions and velocities of the object.

Causality also plays a role in the study of quantum mechanics, which is the branch of physics that studies the behavior of particles on a very small scale. In quantum mechanics, causality is a central principle, but it is also one of the most controversial aspects of the theory. Some interpretations of quantum mechanics suggest that causality is not always a fundamental principle and that particles can be connected in a way that allows for faster-than-light communication.

Finally, the relationship between time and space is also central to the study of cosmology, which is the study of the origin, evolution, and structure of the universe. In cosmology, the idea of time and space as interconnected and relative to the observer is central to our understanding of the large-scale structure of the universe and the origins of the cosmic microwave background radiation. The relationship between time and space is a central aspect of our understanding of the world, and plays a crucial role in many areas of physics and philosophy. The concept of causality, which is based on the idea of time and space as interconnected, is central to our understanding of the laws of motion and the study of quantum mechanics. The relationship between time and space is also central to our understanding of the large-scale structure of the universe in the study of cosmology.

The relationship between time and space is also central to our understanding of consciousness and perception. Consciousness is the awareness of our surroundings and our experiences, and is closely tied to our perception of time. Our perception of time is subjective, meaning that the passage of time can seem to speed up or slow down depending on the observer.

One factor that affects our perception of time is attention. Attention is the process by which we focus our mental resources on a specific task or experience. When we are highly focused and engaged in an activity, time seems to pass more quickly. On the other hand, when we are bored or disengaged, time seems to slow down.

Another factor that affects our perception of time is emotion. Emotional states can have a profound impact on our perception of time, and can cause time to seem to speed up or slow down. For example, when we are experiencing strong emotions such as fear or excitement, time seems to slow down, allowing us to experience the moment more intensely. On the other hand, when we are experiencing more neutral emotions, time seems to pass more quickly.

The relationship between time and space is also central to our understanding of memory. Memory is the process by which we store and retrieve information about our experiences and the world around us. Our perception of time plays a crucial role in our ability to recall memories, as it helps us to organize and categorize our experiences in a way that allows us to retrieve them later. The relationship between time and space is central to our understanding of consciousness, perception, and memory. Our perception of time is subjective, and is affected by factors such as attention and emotion. The relationship between time and space is also central to our ability to recall memories and store information about our experiences. Understanding the relationship between time and space is crucial to our understanding of the world and our place within it.

The relationship between time and space has also been explored in literature, art, and philosophy. In literature, writers often use the manipulation of time and space to create tension, suspense, and to explore deeper themes and ideas. For example, writers often use flashbacks and flash-forwards to explore the past and future and to reveal important information about the characters and the story.

In art, the relationship between time and space is often explored through the use of perspective, which is the technique of representing three-dimensional objects on a two-dimensional surface. Artists use perspective to create the illusion of depth and to manipulate the viewer's perception of time and space. For example, a painting may use perspective to create the illusion of a large, sprawling landscape, even though it is just a small portion of that landscape represented on the canvas.

In philosophy, the relationship between time and space has been the subject of much debate and discussion. Philosophers such as Immanuel Kant and Martin Heidegger have explored the relationship between time and space and the way in which they shape our experiences and understanding of the world. They argue that time and space are not simply objective, neutral concepts, but are inextricably linked to our subjective experiences and the way in which we perceive and interact with the world. In these disciplines, the manipulation of time and space is used to create tension, suspense, and to explore deeper themes and ideas. The relationship between time and space is also central to our understanding of our experiences and our perception of the world, and is the subject of much debate and discussion among philosophers and thinkers. Understanding the relationship between time and space is crucial to our understanding of the world and our place within it.

In physics, the relationship between time and space is central to the theory of special and general relativity. Special relativity, developed by Albert Einstein, argues that the laws of physics are the same for all observers, regardless of their relative velocity. One key aspect of special relativity is the idea that time and space are relative, meaning that they are dependent on the observer's frame of reference. For example, two observers in different frames of reference will experience time differently, and this can affect the way that they perceive the world.

General relativity, also developed by Einstein, builds on the ideas of special relativity and argues that gravity is not a force, but is instead a curvature of spacetime. According to general relativity, the presence of mass or energy causes spacetime to curve, affecting the way that time and space interact with each other. This theory has been confirmed by numerous experiments and observations, and has important implications for our understanding of the universe, including the existence of black holes and the nature of the Big Bang. In physics, the theory of special and general relativity explores the relationship between time and space and how they are affected by relative velocity and gravity. Understanding the relationship between time and space is crucial to our understanding of the world and our place within it, and has important implications for our understanding of the universe.

In psychology, the relationship between time and space has also been studied in regards to how it affects our perceptions and experiences. For example, research has shown that our perception of time can be influenced by our surroundings and the events that are happening around us. For instance, in a stressful or dangerous environment, time can appear to slow down, while in a pleasurable or relaxing environment, time can seem to fly by.

In addition, research has also shown that our perception of time can be affected by our age. As we grow older, our perception of time can change, with time appearing to pass more quickly as we age. This phenomenon has been explained as a result of our brain processing information more quickly as we get older, leading to a faster perception of time.

Understanding how our surroundings and age can affect our perception of time can help us to better understand the world and our place within it. Further research in this area has the potential to shed more light on how we perceive and experience time and space, and how these perceptions and experiences shape our understanding of the world.

In philosophy, the relationship between time and space has been a topic of debate and exploration for centuries. For example, Immanuel Kant argued that time and space are not external realities that exist independently of our perceptions, but are instead subjective and internal to our minds. According to Kant, time and space are necessary conditions for our perception of the world and are used by the mind to order and structure sensory information.

In contrast, the philosopher Henri Bergson argued that time is not simply a mental construct, but is instead a real and flowing reality that exists independently of our perceptions. Bergson argued that time is not divided into fixed and measurable units, but is instead a continuous and flowing experience that is unique to each individual.

Finally, some philosophers have explored the relationship between time and space in relation to the nature of reality. For example, the philosopher Julian Barbour has argued that time is not a fundamental aspect of reality, but is instead a human invention that has been created to help us understand and make sense of the world. According to Barbour, the true nature of reality is timeless, with events happening all at once, rather than in a linear and sequential manner.

The relationship between time and space has been explored

through the theories of relativity and quantum mechanics. In Einstein's theory of relativity, time and space are not separate and distinct entities, but are instead intimately connected and interdependent. According to Einstein, the fabric of space and time are not fixed, but are instead affected by the presence of matter and energy, leading to the phenomenon of time dilation and space curvature.

In quantum mechanics, the relationship between time and space becomes even more complex. According to quantum mechanics, the position and momentum of a particle cannot be known simultaneously, and time and space become entangled in a quantum state. This entanglement means that the relationship between time and space becomes non-linear and non-local, leading to a range of strange and unexpected phenomena, such as quantum entanglement and quantum teleportation.

In cosmology, the relationship between time and space has been explored in the context of the origin and evolution of the universe. According to the Big Bang theory, the universe began as a singularity, with all of space and time compressed into a single point. As the universe expanded, space and time began to separate, leading to the formation of galaxies, stars, and planets.

In conclusion, the relationship between time and space has been explored in a variety of ways in physics, from Einstein's theory of relativity, to quantum mechanics, to cosmology. These theories have had a profound impact on our understanding of the world and have challenged our assumptions about the nature of reality. Further research in these fields has the potential to deepen our understanding of the relationship between time and space and to uncover new and unexpected phenomena.

9 798889 751441

Printed by Libri Plureos GmbH in Hamburg, Germany